TIME YOUR LIFE

By

Rev. William Okyere

For details about other books by author and speaking arrangements please contact him on:

+233 (0) 557 581 505

email: pneumeduf@gmail.com.

ISBN: 978-9988-0-9175-0
© 2001
Pastor William Okyere

Printed & Published by:
Pastor William Okyere
Tel: +233 (0) 557 581 505
pneumeduf@gmail.com.
All rights reserved.

Dedicated to

The Youth of Ghana

ACKNOWLEDGMENT

I wish to express my sincere thanks to the Almighty God who has sustained me through the difficulties of life so I could share my knowledge and experiences in this life with others.

I also want to acknowledge the effort of Mrs. Joyce Danso, of Christian Action Faith Ministries, who first typed the material. She did not only typeset this material but also read through and provided fruitful suggestions to bring this work this far. Thanks Auntie Joyce.

I am also grateful to Mrs. Doris Korley, Ex-Head Teacher of Manna Mission Academy, for reading through the script.

Another thanks to Emmanuel who retyped this very edition because we lost the software of the first print.

Very special thanks to Alice, my wife for the hard work and support in helping raise our children (Christie-Ann, Mike, Gabby and Ayeyi), so I can make to do other things.

TABLE OF CONTENTS

TIME

INTRODUCTION

We know and appreciate the fact that God, the Almighty, has bestowed on mankind many blessings. Our problem is that we never have been able to count our blessings and name them one by one as the hymn writer admonishes us to do. Because few ever realize the wonderful providence of God, few are therefore thankful to Him.

One of such unappreciated blessings is (the span of) time. Time, as defined by Dr. Myles Monroe, is the accumulation of moments. It is, however, not just the passing away of moments; it is God's plan. God, I believe, has spread His blessings designed for each man over our lifetime. For the Bible says His mercies are new every morning; They span our lifetime. (*Lamentation 3:22*) And therefore as moments pass, God's plan of blessing for our lives keeps unfolding. Our appreciation of time therefore is our appreciation of God's blessings. The Christian's time is therefore God's time.

When the believer dedicates his time to God, He (God) makes all things beautiful in His time. (Eccl. 3:11)

It was God who set the times and the seasons. (*Gen 8:22*) so important was time to God that He set rulers over it.

> **Then God said, let there be light in the firmament of the Heavens to divide the day from the night; and let them be for signs and seasons, and for days and years; then God made two lights: the greater to rule the day and the lesser to rule the night... (Gen 1:14, 16)**

The scripture we just read indicates that time must carefully be observed and analyzed so as to put it to a better use. One way of doing this is to ask ourselves why so much happen during the day? It is because God gave the day more opportunities; to the day God gave greater light. No wonder Jesus, in emphasizing the busyness of his commission, said that he must work whilst it is '**day**'. (*John 9:4*) God gave the day a greater light and the night, a lesser one. Common sense will tell you that much can be accomplished in the day than in the night. Experience teaches that all things will not prosper equally at all times. There are times in one's life that can be called the day and other times can be described as night. This book will guide us to do our best during the day of our lives and do the appropriate when it is night.

Assessing times and seasons therefore is a whole field of study and that is what we, in a small way, are attempting to do in this little book, may I outline few of the many blessings that putting time to good use brings to us:

TIME BRINGS IMPROVEMENT

Come, Osofo (Pastor), say hello to auntie is a regular utterance that my mother makes any time I visit my village. Then comes my auntie's turn; *"who is this, your last baby? I can't believe this. The last time I saw him he was a toddler*. What is the gap between the last time and today? **TIME**. Time really improves situations. Anything or any situation that has time invested into it improves. The reason many families are breaking up is that they hardly make time for each other. Families need time to improve. Our walk with God and our service to Him, be it full time ministry, general Christian leadership or any other aspect and at any level, needs time to improve. Time is not only needed for our pursuit of economic survival. It is unfortunate that time is only valued when it comes to economic survival.

Time also improves our perception of life and its related issues. That is why the elderly are expected to be wiser; Why? More time has gone into their lives. It is worth prioritizing our time in such a way that the areas that need special attention receive quality time. An example is the lifelong journey of marriage. Whilst it takes almost one's entire youth and energetic life to prepare for a profession one can, and many do, abandon at any time, many couples devote less than three months, and some even days, to prepare a for a marriage that is to last for the rest one's life; never to be abandoned. Many will pursue special professional upgrades, but hardly any such thing for marriage. Why do you think our marriages are struggling to survive? No time.

There is a more permanent relationship that travels beyond marriage. One's relationship with God is to span one's entire earthly life and beyond. Eternity is the word. It means in terms of time allotment our spiritually must be the number one.

However, it is most often the last item. The average Christian spends about 30 minutes a day for God in terms of devotional life and about six hours a week in terms of co-operate worship. So, in a week, the average Christian spends about ten hours on spirituality. What it means is that if one's adult life span from 18 years to 70 years, it means that out of the 52 years of one's life comprising of 455,808 hours, only 27,040 was allocated to one's eternal relationship with God and that makes it a total of 6% of one's entire adult life. Yet we claim to love God with all our heart. We still could have made this up by making Him the center of all other life endeavors but no, He is shut out of them. Well it is even possible that proceeds from our professional efforts are given to the spreading of God`s kingdom. So, let`s assume in all we commit 10% of our entire life to the things of God. That is, if we are consistent with our devotions and church attendance all through our adult lives. The question is, Should the most important aspect of our lives be given only 10% attention? No wonder our spiritual lives today are getting shallower and shallower. The one area in which we excel in our commitment to God is in the area of singing it.

All to Jesus I surrender

All to him I freely give

I will ever love and trust Him

In His presence daily live

If our commitment to God is measured by the way we sing it, that would have been very perfect. God told the Israelites, You serve me with your lips, but your heart is far from me. *(Matt. 15:8)*

It is true we sincerely need some material things to survive. That one alone attracts a chunk of our time. The question is, Do we need God to survive? If yes, then why is it that issues relating to our relationship with God is not attracting the quality of time we give to other needs.

It will interest every Christian to know that the main reason why Jesus came to die is to draw the believer closer to God.

All things are of God, who reconciled us to Himself by Jesus Christ, and hath given us the ministry of reconciliation. That is, that God was in Christ reconciling the world to Himself, not imputing their trespasses unto them; and had committed unto us the ministry 0f reconciliation. *(2 Corinthians 5:18, 19)*

It is obvious that many believers are doing so much for God. However, Christianity is not how much of things we give to God but rather how much of ourselves we give to Him. Neither is it how much of God we give to others but how much of ourselves we give to Him. It is not how much we do for Him it is how much we do with Him.

TIME HEALS

Time is one of the greatest sources of healing that God has given man. We are constantly advised not to react to provocation immediately they happen, simply because the more the wind of time blows over issues and situations, the higher the probability of anger and bitterness subsiding. Any time I go through a difficult situation, I soothe my emotional pain by projecting my vision to the future when all will be over. Because I know they surely will. This brings me a lot of consolation because I know time heals and improves situations. Time indeed carries solutions. This is particularly true to the Christian because our redemption draws closer with time. No matter how difficult life looks, we are getting closer to our redemption, Better days are ahead. Hallelujah! At the same the wicked person is moving towards destruction. Time brings the Christian hope. Don`t give up. No don`t. For as long as we are in Christ, we can hope for glory *(Colossians 1:27)*

But we all, with unveiled face, beholding as in a mirror the glory of the lord, are being translated into the same image from GLORY TO GLORY (2 Corinthians 3:18)

The Christian life is spread with the glory of God and as long as we live worthy as Christians our future remains glorious. God has not designed it for the Christian to retrogress; the Christian walk is an upward call. *(Hebrews 3 :1)*

Many times, we all look back and ask ourselves, How could we have gone through that? At that time, we did not believe we could go through what we did but with time we did. God`s grace did it with time. The Bible promises the Christian a better future under the most adverse of conditions:

"My brethren, count it all joy when ye fall into various trials, knowing that the testing of your faith produces patience. But let patience have its perfect work, that ye may be perfect and complete, lacking nothing." (James 1:2-4)

God is a healing God. He causes all things to work together for our good. The Bible does not say all things are good though. However, God is able to put both the bad the good together for our good. *(Romans 8:28)* God comforts us when we go through difficult times so that with time, we are blessed with so much comfort with which we can comfort others who go through such difficult times too. *(2 Corinthians 1:4).*

We do not seriously think about it when a divorcee talks about relation with a previous spouse, We are still the best of friends. In fact, if you see us interacting with each other, you will not believe something of this sort has happened between us . Yes, it does happen because time can really heal sour relationships, emotional hurts and their related pains. The only challenge is that such couple could not wait for time to arrive with healing within the marriage. Too bad healing came when the wrong decision had already been taken. If a couple could be the best of friends in divorce, they possibly could have been same, or better, within marriage. We must allow the wind of time to blow over the most infuriating of   situations. Time gives us understanding concerning issues and it also helps our emotions to settle so that we can allow true wisdom to act.

TIME IS AN OPEN SPACE TO BE FILLED

Time is an open field to be cultivated. One`s today is the result of his yesterday and one`s tomorrow will be the result of his today. one`s use of time must be guided by the principle of sowing and reaping: whatever a man sows that he reaps.*(Gal. 6:7b)*

No doubt many are thinking about continuing their education and searching for ways to improve their lives. Unfortunately, many others are still bound by their past and therefore, plan their courses of action according to the past. For example, someone may be thinking about how to revenge a stepmother who denied him the opportunity to attend a better school. Such thoughts continually fill their lives and minds with the intention to revenge; hardly leaving any room for the positive issues of life. There is so much hope in this life in the midst of all the difficulties, but many are not looking towards the direction of hope because they are tightly holding on to the past. You cannot hold on to the past and look another direction; no, it is impossible. What does it mean for one to hold on so much to unfortunate calamities of life? He must be excused for everything that goes wrong in his life and another or something must be blamed for it. It also means the person is walking backwards though he seems to be moving forward. It so happens that many fill their future with negatives instead of thinking about what they can do to rectify the past by learning valuable lessons... We can undo the harm others have done by bringing forth the good from within us.

"I returned and saw under the sun, that the race is not to the swift, nor the battle to the strong neither yet bread t the wise, nor yet riches to men of understanding, nor yet favor to men of skill; but TIME and CHANCE hapeneth to them all. (Ecclesiastes 9:11)

He that unduly dwells on what others have done has lost sight of what he can do. God decorates us with different capabilities as we come into this world. That is what Solomon is saying with the above scripture. It simply means that we all come into this world with different talents and capabilities; some are strong, others swift; he may be very wise, another with understanding and others with favor. Whatever one has, God has given each one of us time to improve upon them. The word `chance' here implies that success is a possibility. We can call time a factory of futures.

The attitudes and the thought patterns with which we fill it will determine our tomorrow. Are we filling this factory with raw materials that will determine our tomorrow bright or things that make us worse than we are today? When we fill our lives with worry today, we must not expect happiness tomorrow. Worry can only take away our joy; it does not add up to it. *(Matt.6:25-34)* God, the Great Teacher, having given us this great gift of time, has also given us in His word, an accurate instruction as to how time is to be managed. Human life can be compared to the earth from which we were formed. When the rains have not fallen, the earth looks all dust and sand. When it is that dry, we hardly see any vegetation on the ground. The whole system however changes when the rains begin to fertilize the earth, then one realizes that under the dry earth were seeds of life that were only waiting for the rain to germinate to become a whole vegetation. Places nobody thought could germinate with weeds surprise us the most. Even foot paths that had been hardened by human footprints begin to grow weeds especially when they are no more used as such. A situation may need only one rain from heaven to become a 'fertilized land'. It is important for us to redirect our thoughts towards heaven for its dew to fertilize us. We do not need to concentrate on the negative past as if there is no hope for tomorrow.

TIME IS MONEY

Many young people do not know how wealthy they are. They have a lot time in their life account and if it is true that time is money then it must be true that the youth are wealthy. The challenge is that time is not directly money. It is a raw material that when placed in the factory of skill and guidance, money can be one of the end products.

People are paid according to how well they have invested their time and/or how much time they are given to invest into.

I have intentionally placed an appendix of how much time everyone has depending on the number of years one has to live on earth I encourage every young man reading this book to check an hourly or daily wage and multiply it by the number of working years one has left and that young person will realize how wealthy he or she is. Many of our youth do not realize that their lives now are attracting a wage that will be paid by them tomorrow. Let's imagine two young people on their way to their futures: One decides to put his life to skillful use; the other sits behind the TV many hours a day. One works so hard to complete his education to an appreciable level or learns a trade whilst the other is always exchanging DVDs. At a certain time, they all seek employment in a particular company. One is unskilled; the other, fully skilled. The difference between the wages of the skilled and unskilled relates to the time better spent many years ago.

What is means that, at a certain stage in life, you will not pay your life's investments until at a later stage; let's say, on the job. So, the question should be, Are my efforts today labor worthy tomorrow? Many people today are being paid for the educational and apprenticeship efforts of yesterday as well as their current skills and efforts.

Every life has a seed. Time is one of life's seeds God has given to man. Sow your seed on a fertile ground or a yielding soil; do not throw it anywhere. Do not be deceived, God is not mocked. Whatever a man sows that is what he reaps.(Gal 6:7)

As the earth remains there will always be seedtime and harvest.(Genesis 8:22) when we sow and water the seeds with our tears we will harvest and put them in baskets of joy. (Psalm 126:5)

TIME IS EXHAUSTIBLE

Have you ever seen someone biting his finger? Had I known , How do we feel if we are slapped with the statement, I am sorry, it is too late . Once travelling to Cameroun on one of Africa's airlines, one passenger got so hungry after the flight was delayed for so long. Finally, he decided to take off his mind from the situation by reading the contents on his travelling documents. It was then that he found out that his ticket was accompanied by a coupon for free lunch. Just as he started asking for where the restaurant was, there was announcement for the passengers to proceed to the boarding gate. Too late. Had food in his hand all the time he was hungry. Life is filled with such examples. It is not always what we do but doing what we do at the right time.

We always get behind time because we do not treat time as exhaustible. The parable of the ten virgins that will be discussed later helps us to understand that many situations provide early opportunities for clearing a mess, rectifying a crumbling situation and preventing a disaster from escalating. How painful it is when such begging opportunities pass us by without even noticing them.

 Many look up to second chances which the merciful Lord, on several occasions, provides. However, many 'second chances' come our way as best chances before the unfortunate happens. The real second chance is the one that is preventive and not a curatives type. God loves it when we forestall a disaster before it happens. Curative situations are not the best. Even temptations, prominent as they are among humans, are to be prevented. Jesus admonishes believers to watch and pray so that we do not fall into temptation. *(Matthew 26:41)*

The relationship between time and disaster is that a brief period of negligence can cause a major disaster. One does not need a long period to be destructive or to waste precious resources through unprofitable ventures. On the other hand, one needs much time to do the positive or to build. To be constructive is more demanding than to be destructive. It is therefore important for the constructive to mop up every day available time and use them effectively to achieve his goal. We must use all available means to prevent the necessity of rebuilding and restoration in our lives, because they are very expensive, timewise.

It can take one`s whole life to recover from drug addiction. So, the best use of time is to make every effort not to get involve in with the negative. It can be very demanding to try to overcome a bad habit that has been cultivated. Why then did you have to cultivate it in to in the first place? What Satan can do with the little time we give him will be discussed later in the book. Time is exhaustible and retrieved it from a bad habit can be expensive.

 if you had a bank account that credited your account each morning with $86,400, that carried no balance from day to day, allowed you to keep no cash in your account and finally every evening cancelled whatever part of the amount you had failed to use during the day, what would you do? Draw out every cent of course.

Well you have such a bank and its name is 'Time' opens new accounts with you. Each night it burns the records of the day. If you fail to use the day's deposits, the loss is yours, (Robert Gee Lee)

TIME FLIES

Time is not only exhaustible, it flies. When it is ahead of you, it looks very slow in passing but when it is behind you, you easily realize its speed.

That is why the adult is more cautious about life; they can predict by their experience that they do not have much time left. Life runs fast and therefore makes it brief.

"You have made my days a mere hand breath; the span of my years is as nothing before you. Each man's life is but a breath. *(Psalm 39:5)*. Looking back, 50 years ago just look like yesterday. Time flew pass us. It passes unnoticed unless it is identified by a memoir. It is always a healing process to insert activities that will be precious memories tomorrow, into time.

This is what makes procrastination a deadly disease. Time waits for no man. It does not mean we must necessarily be running in life, but it means we must invest well into situations that are timeless, our spiritual lives and our relationships must have time well invested into them. A precious moment shared with a loved one will remain as long as life lasts.

"The length of our days is seventy years or eighty…for they quickly pass, and we fly away. Teach us to number our days aright, that we may gain a heart of wisdom" *(Psalm 90:12)*

TIME CAN BE "MULTIPLIED"

Today many of the things that took us months to do can be done in hours. Before the invention of the airplane we traveled by ship and it took us months to travel from one nation to the other. Today in thirteen hours one can travel from Amsterdam to Guatemala City . Someone would describe the situation as saving time but on the other hand, it can also be described as multiplying time. Through skillful use of time, one can achieve in a day what another can achieve in three weeks. The keys to multiplying time is skill and excellence. Why do we train? To do things skillfully and excellently. Definitely when time multiplies income also multiplies. For if one accomplishes in a way what others are accomplishing in three weeks then it means that one can make an income in one day what others are making in three weeks. Skill will 'multiply` our income because it will multiply up our time.

An incident is told of Daniel Webster that at one time a poor man came to him for advice relative to a rather intricate case. Mr. Webster sent out for legal books that cost him considerable money, more than his client finally paid him when the case was won. Years later, Aaron Burr called to see Mr. Webster, placing before him a will case which baffled the former. Mr. Webster helped him through and in a few words, made the situation clear to his celebrated colleague. 'Wonderful`, exclaimed Mr. Burr, 'Wonderful knowledge of law! I cannot understand it!' Then Mr. Webster told him that he had a similar case some time ago. In less than five minutes of a legal advice, Mr. Webster charged Mr. Burr $500.00(five hundred dollars) The knowledge that had been stored in that brain for all those years was now ready to receive its wage," *(C.E. World)*

Developing a skill can be expensive today but it will definitely pay off tomorrow. On a lighter note; a patient complained bitterly, "Three hundred dollars is a lot of money for pulling a tooth in less than five minutes". "Well" replied the dentist consolingly, "If you wish, I can pull it very slowly.

CHAPTER 1

WALKING CIRCUMSPECTLY

That is why it is said: "Wake up , O sleeper, rise from the dead, and Christ will shine on you..."See then that you walk circumspectly, not as fools, but as wise, Redeeming the time, because the days are evil." (Ephesians 5:14 -16)

The key to the effective analysis of the above passage lies in carefully observing the following words contained in it: awake, sleep, arise, dead, light, circumspect, fools, wise, redeem, time, evil. These words actually summarize all that we will be discussing. The passage starts by calling the sleeping to arise. Many are closing their eyes to the realities of life. They are therefore fast asleep in despair and hopelessness. Why the wake-up call? God does not give light to the sleeping because the sleeping rather needs darkness to sleep.

We will never see light until we have woken up from such sleep. Light is only available to the active. Many are waiting for light before they wake up. Naturally, men wake up as they see the daybreak but spiritually God withholds His light until we have woken up.

"Thy word is a lamp unto my feet and a light unto my path." (Psalm 119:105)

God gives light to only the feet that create the path. Knowledge and wisdom grow by consistent application of truth. Applying truth brings forth more truth and equips us with higher skills to further apply truth. Truth loses its value when it is not practiced. It is better to know little and put it into practice than to read volumes of books and be stacked as the books from which one gained the knowledge from.

Truth is light and anyone who has it cannot live as one under the influence of darkness- sleeping. This is because when we sleep in irresponsibility, we are as good as dead. And also remember that, in this life we do not escape evil by sleeping from it, we walk over evil by standing face to face to it:

"Finally, my brethren, be strong in the Lord, and in the power of His might. Put on the whole amour of God that ye may be able to stand against the wiles of the devil." (Ephesians 6:10, 11)

It is only by truth that we can fight the battles of life effectively. And until we apply biblical truth to time management, we are on our way to defeat. Because, of all that we possess in life, the enemy is most interest in our time.

Division of our time in our lives has thus been sketched by Dr. C.C. Albertson. "There are 168 hours in each week. Fifty-six of these we spend in sleep. Of the remaining 112 hours, we devote 48 to labor. This leaves sixty-four hours of which twelve hours is assigned for daily meals. (This allows thirty-minutes for each meal, and one and half hours to promote good digestion) we have left fifty-two hours net of conscious active life to devote any purpose to which we are inclined. Is it too much to say that God requires a tithe of this true time? Our tenth of fifty-two hours is 5.2 hours. How much of this tithe of time do we devote to strictly religious (spiritual) uses?

The Christian does not fight a strong devil; only a tricky one. This therefore calls for circumspective living. 'Circum - 'is a prefix, meaning 'around' and the other half of the word is from a Latin word spectaculum which means 'to watch'. From that root word we have we have a word like 'spectator or spectacular. Walking circumspectly therefore means looking around before you take a walk. In ordinary words, "be careful." A good example is what we see in films when a man enters a house with a gun attempting to shoot someone but also cautious that someone may also be in that house also trying to shoot. In such a situation any step he/she takes, he first makes sure he is safe. This is depicted in *1 Peter 5:8: "Be sober, be vigilant, because you adversary the devil, as a roaring lion, walketh about seeking whom he may devour"*

Isn't it amazing? That is exactly what the Lord created the earth to do. As the earth moves in its orbit, it is turning around watching all that is going on around her. Interestingly this style of movement is, in every way, related to time. The earth moves on its orbit as it rotates on its axis. The complete rotation on its axis is done in twenty-four hours making a day whilst a complete revolution on its orbit is done in 365 and a quarter day giving us one year. God is therefore telling us to do what His earth does, move but do so cautiously.

The Bible never leaves us in the dark as to how best we can walk circumspectly. In verse 16 of Ephesians chapter 5, the Bible clearly states that we can do this by redeeming the time.

It is interesting to note that the same word used for Christ redeeming our souls is used here. What then is the theological meaning of the term 'redemption'? The Biblical concept of redemption always means payment of price to recover from the power or control of another.

Redemption therefore simply means 'being set free from slavery'. The Greek term 'exagorazo' is made up of two words; 'ex' meaning 'out' and 'agorazo' meaning 'slave market'. Redemption therefore emphasizes being set free out of the slave market never to be sold as a slave again. Nobody ever came out of slave market free without the price tag on him not fully settle. To have our souls redeemed, Christ had to pay the full price. This is what is called 'ransom'. So, *1 Corinthians 6:20 says: "For ye are bought with a price: therefore, glorify God in your body and in your spirit, which are God's. "So important and costly was our redemption that only the blood of Christ could pay:*

"For even the son of man came not to be ministered unto, but to minister, and to give His life a ransom for many."(Mark 10:45)

With this background the following conclusions can be deduced from *Ephesians 5:16:*

1. That whilst Christ redeems our souls, He has placed into our own hands the responsibility of redeeming our own time. Christ redeems our souls; you redeem your time. And just as Christ paid a price for souls, you cannot attempt to redeem your time without the readiness to pay a price. Whenever there is responsibility there is accountability. This means we will have to give account before God one day as to how we used the time He blessed us with. Of course, our motivation to make good use of time should not only be influenced by this caution but also by the opportunities that emanate from making good use of our time.

2. It also implies that whilst Christ has purchased the believer's soul from the slave market of sin, his/her time may still be on the slave market of laziness, worry, bitterness, watching TV, complaining and many others. It may differ from person to person. Men, (Christians not excluded) can be occupied with very unproductive

activities. This is what the devil wants us to. In that case, he does not need to fight us. He encourages us to create our own opponents from within us; What he achieves by this is to make us our own enemies. The devil deceives us by making us create battles within ourselves.

Dear Christian, what occupies you? Your Bible is lying down waiting to be read; there is a prayer to be said, there is a worship to ascend to heaven; there may be a hymn to be sung; there is an intercession to do. What are you doing now?

" Said yesterday to tomorrow
When I was young like you
I, too, was fond of boasting of all I meant to do
But while I fell a-dreaming along the pleasant way
Before I scarcely knew it.
I found it was today
And as to-day, so quickly
My little cause was run
I had no time to finish
One half the things began
Would I could try it over
But I can never go back
Yesterday for ever,
I now must be alack
And so, my good tomorrow,
If you would make a name
That history shall cherish
Upon its roll of fame
Be all prepared and ready
Your noblest part to play
In those new fleeting hours
When you shall be 'today'".

The Pacific

The reason, according to the Bible, why we should redeem our time is that the days are evil. It does not mean the earlier times where less evil. What it means is that Satan has a strategy against our generation too. It also means it is not only God that works in a dispensational manner, Satan does too. It was violent persecution in the early church period, and some other times in other places, it seems to be, basically, the infiltration of seemingly unharmful worldliness and discontentment in our days. The Christian's greatest threat today is not persecution, it is purposelessness.

"Little children, it is the last time as ye have heard that the anti-Christ shall come, even now are there many antichrists; whereby we know it is the TIME".(1 John 2:18)

This confirms that as the end draws closer Satan changes his strategy against the world. Satan is making different use of his time in these last days in which we live by misdirecting many Christians from the real essentials of life. In our days we are praying less, we are taking our devotional lives less seriously and Television and the internet has become our god. The devil does not need to attack us in all areas of our lives. If he succeeds in getting us to use time wrongly, he is in control of all the other areas of our lives. The Christian who will abuse time therefore is in danger of being overtaken by the enemy.

3. Satan does not need a lot of time to destroy. Just give him 15 minutes and he can prove to you that he is an efficient time manager. It may take one the rest of his life t to restore what Satan destroys in his life in fifteen minutes. That is what Jesus meant by saying, "sufficient unto the day is the evil thereof "*(Matt 6:34)*. In other words, all the harm Satan means to cause in our lives can be accomplished in a day. So instead of worrying about tomorrow, think about today because if Satan takes hold of you today, he is in control of your tomorrow as well. Jesus never meant we should not pray or think about the future but rather that our attention for today compared to that of tomorrow should never be the same . Tomorrow has not yet come so work with what you have; pray and watch against all the possible evil that may work against you. Besides, today came with a lot of opportunities; do not let them go. So, in the Lord's prayer, Jesus taught us to for our daily bread (opportunities) and also deliverance from evil. Paul, emphasizing the same point, also said that we should not give the devil a place in our lives. *(Ephesians 4:27)*

Let us have the following for an example:

Tom Young is jobless and therefore has resorted to worrying ; not doing any constructive thing to redeem his time. Instead of finding something in the Church to do as a Christian, to make him feel useful in a way, he rather feels disappointed by God and the fact that the Church is not giving him money to solve some of his financial problems. He therefore decides to stop going to church . After all, his outfits are getting worn— out and unfortunately no church member is helping him out. When his old friends realized that Tom is no more attending church, they started visiting him. The old influence was gradually returning. He has begun again to see nothing wrong with drinking, especially when he is not using his own money to buy it. *"make sure you do not fall into gutter", becomes his motto. On one of such idle day comes Jack Push.*

"Good news, Tom", he says, "I have won lottery. Let's go and celebrate.". To the nearest bar they go. Just at a time they had gotten a little tipsy, a fully drunk, man comes and begins to insult them for no apparent reason. A little confrontation develops and before **Tom** realizes, he has broken a beer bottle and stabbed this 'tempter' to death. All these may have taken place in a very short period but under the law, Tom may have to pay for this for the rest of his entire life. This is an example of a situation that can hardly be rectified. The Christian indeed is to remain prayerful for the days are evil.

CHAPTER 2

THE EPHESIAN ANTIDOTE

So, what do I do to manage my time the God-glorifying way? one may ask. Interestingly the Ephesians' passage *(5:15, 16)* discussed in the previous chapter did not leave us in the dark as to how to redeem our time. This passage gives us two ways by which we can redeem our time:

1. UNDERSTANDING WHAT THE WILL OF THE LORD IS

There cannot be a purposeful or meaningful Christian living without knowing the will of the Lord. Purposelessness is a great disadvantage to Satan. Satan always meets Christians on the 'walk about ' street, because he also walks about *(1 Peter 5: 8)*. The Christian who just walks about is sure to fall into the hands of the devil. It is very expensive to lead a trial-and-error Christian life. We must consciously plan our lives in all areas. We must even plan our spiritual activities; when we want to read our Bible and those important details. The author of this book can be contacted for a Bible reading guide and a prayer Journal.

The will of God is an essential commodity in our walk with God. Satan knows it will go against him to attempt to make the believer think that the will of God is not necessary. If Satan ever whispered such a thought, the believer will instantly identify where the thought is coming from. What Satan does therefore is to offer us counterfeits in the name of the will of God. He therefore presents himself as an angel of light. (*2 Corinthians 11:14)*

It is unfortunate that many Christians today, receive every seeming opportunity as a blessing from God. We commit our efforts into situations only to find out at the end that it was not of God. Many have entered into relationships that promise to be safe but have ruined their lives. If only we can wait on God for a while, we could have our future secure.

Because God belongs to the spiritual domain it is impossible to identify His ways physically. Many times, what may seem right to us may lead us to destruction.

(Proverbs 14:12) Except we watch and pray, the devil will always offer counterfeits for God's will. What has this got to do with redeeming our time? Everything! The Christian cannot continue a genuine cause on a counterfeit foundation. Many ordeals we can save ourselves from, if we regularly consult God for His guidance. The Christian therefore should spend time to seek the will of God. I know the question that is running through your mind; ' how do I identify the will of God?' For sure this is a difficult question, instead of giving you a direct answer, here are some important guideline.

1. Basically, whatsoever is of God gets the Christian closer to God. God's number one aim is to get His children closer to Him. That is why Jesus came. Christians therefore should be careful of the things that draw us further away from God. God will not place us where the intensity of our Bible study, Christian commitment, prayer life and fellowship will drop. In seeking the will of God, therefore, sort out between the things that draw you closer to God and the things that drive you further away from.

2. Whatever is of God will produce fruits even if it is very difficult to pursue. What fruits are we talking about? They are many and various but by fruit we primarily mean anything that will bring glory to the name to God. God will never lead us to do anything that will bring shame to His name. We should never forget that we are witnesses and therefore any step we take must draw us to God and draw others to God as well.

Our testimonies can cause even those who refuse to be drawn to Him to give glory to the God of Heaven. *(Matthew 5:16)*

There is therefore no better way of spending our time than drawing closer to God and by glorifying His name because the days are evil. God's will is available to those who seek it. The prerequisite is the desire to know His will. *(James 1:5)*

John Stott, in his book, *The contemporary Christian*, outlines five steps one must follow to discover the will of God:

1. Yield – Surrender Your Will (Matthew 26:39)

2. Pray – (James 4:2)

3. Talk — Seek counsel from other mature believers (Prov 13:10)

4. Think — Weigh up the pros and the cons. (1 Corinthians 6:12)

5. Wait — It is always wise to wait when not certain. (Proverbs 21: 5)

The book of Ephesians has given us one keyway of redeeming our time; Understanding the will of the Lord.

The second key, found in the book of Ecclesiastes, is **APPROPRIATE TIME APPORTIONING.** This is pursuing what God Himself does; He has apportioned times and seasons for everything;

"To everything there is a season and a time to every purpose under the heaven: A time to be born, and a time to die; a time to plant, and to time to pluck up that which was planted; A time kill, and a time to heal; a time to break down and a time to build up; A time to weep, and a time to laugh; a time to mourn and a time to dance; a time to cast away stones and a time to gather stones together ; a time to embrace and a time to refrain from embracing; a time to get and a time to lose; a time to keep and a time to cast away; a time to rend, and a time to sew; a time to keep silence and a time to speak ; a time to love and a time to hate; a time of war and a time of peace." (Ecclesiastics 3:8)

Scripture is very time conscious. The Bible evidently extols promptness in attitude. There is always the best time for everything under the sun. "I must work the work of Him that sent me whilst it is day; the night comes when no man can work." *(John 9:4)*

"Remember now thy creator in the days of thy youth, while evil days come not, nor the years draw nigh. (Ecclesiastics 12: 1) "Because of laziness, the building decays, and through idleness of hands the house leaks. "(Ecclesiastes 12:8) We must be prompt in the things we do and how we respond to changing situations.

We are not necessarily talking about rushing; we are talking about readiness to act when the opportunity manifests itself.

We cannot have war at time there is to be peace. The time for war was the time we belonged to the kingdom of the devil. Now is the time for peace. The time for constant mourning was the time we were under the influence of the wicked. Now our souls have escaped, as a bird, out of the snare of the fowler. The snare is broken, and we are escaped; our help is in the name of the Lord.*(Psalm 124:7, 8)* This is the time for dancing; we should not go back to mourning. For Isaiah explains the time for dancing;

"Therefore, the redeemed of the Lord shall return, and come with singing unto Zion; and everlasting joy shall be upon their heads: they shall obtain gladness and joy; and sorrow and mourning shall flee away." (Isaiah 51:11)

Things done in their right time brings much benefit. When things are not done in their most appropriate timing, their effectiveness minimizes. For example, the Bible says,

"Train up a child in the way he should go, and when he old, he would not depart from it."(Proverbs 22: 6)

The most effective stage for training is the childhood stage. Unfortunately, many will wait till their children are married before they start training them. By this time, they have already been 'trained'. As for the one who did the 'training', time will tell. When did this training take place? one may ask; it always takes place when , as parents, we are busy running around, chairing social functions and leaving our children in the care of house helps, security men and next-door neighbors.

This training stage for children and youth stage is also the best time for traditional education. However, many teenagers mess their lives around and only realize the importance of education when they are 36 years. Some, at this stage, may try to get some education but this time cannot compete with the original timing. Why? At the early stage of life, all things being equal, parents sponsor the education whilst the child does the learning, but at a later stage one has to do both sponsoring and learning at the same time plus other responsibilities like also sponsoring one's own children's education. Time is precious; to waste it is to lose pearls: *"Yet a little sleep, a little slumber, a little folding of the hands to sleep; so shall thy poverty come as the one that traveleth; and thy want as an armed man". (Prov 24:33, 34)*

Indeed, a lazy man's needs are unconquerable. Because the major way God has designed to have our needs met is to work. There is no alternative to hard work. Many do not realize that another word for blessing is work. Many 'good' Christians unfortunately think that work is the result of the curse. That is not true, Biblically, before the curse came, there was work. In fact, the reason why God gave the first couple work to do was because He had blessed them.

"And God blessed them, and God said unto them, be fruitful and multiply, and replenish the earth, and subdue it; and have dominion over the fish of the sea, and over the foul of the air, and over every living thing that moves upon the earth." *(Genesis 1:28).*

The Bible gives a vivid picture about the tiniest of creatures that is able to overcome its need- the ant. What is its secret? The ant understands that there is a season for abundance in life and another for scarcity. This is God's law:

"Whilst the earth remaineth, seed time and harvest, cold and heat, and summer and winter, and day and night shall never cease." (Genesis 8:32)

Many fail to realize that there are some special occasions when we can gather a little more against lean seasons. Such times call for doing a little extra to store up against the lean season. This is what the scripture says about the ant.

"Go to the ant thou sluggard; consider her ways, and be wise: which having no guide, overseer, or ruler provideth her meat in the summer, and gathereth her food in the harvest."(Proverbs 6:6, 7).

Many are able to gather up a little extra in abundant seasons but fail in storing up for the lean season and therefore return to lack in times of difficulty. The reason is that many do not consider the poss**ibility of a lean** season. Actually, if the ant principle is followed, there will not be a lean season because wisdom can keep us abounding in lean seasons. Many in this world have no excuse for their poverty because they have once lived in abundance.

 Their only problem is that they did not prepare for a change of season. They probably did not seriously consider the fact that time changes. Different times calls for different responses.

What are some of the ways we can prepare for the lean season?

1. We can invest in viable projects.

2. We can buy insurance policies.

3. We can sow seeds in others' lives and trust God to bless us in times of need.

4. We can honor God with our first fruits and tithes.

5. We can buy properties worth re-selling in times of need.

6. We can buy shares

It is obvious that one of the greatest managers that saved his world at the time used this ant principle:

"Let pharaoh do this, and let him appoint officers over the land, and take up the fifth part of the land in the seven plenteous years. And let them gather all the food of these good years that come, and lay up corn under the hand of pharaoh, and let them keep food in the cities. And that food shall be for store to the land against the seven years of famine, which shall be in the land of Egypt; that the land perishes not through the famine."(Genesis 41:34-36).

It is also interesting that the God who revealed this dream to pharaoh could have decided to give abundant rains instead of the seven lean seasons. Or Joseph could have advised pharaoh that "Let us pray when the famine starts". At this instance God, the Almighty, decided not to change the weather but to give man wisdom as to how handle the situation. Many Christians squander good opportunities today in the name of prayer tomorrow. We do not need to always pray for new miracles.

Consistently we already have so many miracles in our lives. What we rather need to do is to pray for wisdom to effectively manage those miracles already given to us. Besides, miracles happen only when the regular fails. Even the regular is still a miracle. We should not take daily routines for granted. This is the reason why we must be thankful for even the water we drink. They still come every day as miracles. If one ever walks through the desert for only a day without water and finally comes across an oasis, then that person will understand that regular water supply is a regular miracle.

God rained down manna for the Israelites when they journeyed through the wilderness because their nomadic life could not allow regular farming. The moment they got to the promised land where they could farm, the manna ceased falling. God will not rain down manna when we have many opportunities around us unexploited.

Managing wealth and that of time are closely related. Abundant seasons are simply the best or appropriate time. Such seasons do not always exist. They come periodically. Let's look up for such seasons and make the best use of them.

If one lives to be 70 years of age and is an average person, he spends:
20 years sleeping
20 years working
6 years eating
7 years playing
5 years dressing
2 1/2 years pursuing other pleasures
3 Years waiting for somebody
5 years tying shoes
2 1/2 for other things including 1 1/2 years in church.

How much time do you spend doing free night calls? How much time do you sit in front of the TV? How much quality time do you spend arguing about footballers most of who spend their quality time pursuing worldly pleasures? How much time do you spend worrying about a wasted penalty kick whilst the waster is receiving tens of thousands of dollars at the time you are worrying?

CHAPTER 3

UNDERSTANDING THE TIMES

It is one thing to know that there are different seasons and another thing to identify the seasons as they come. Many times, they are even shrouded in adverse circumstances. At other times they are so clear it becomes a mystery when we miss such opportunities. I want you to enroll in the school which will teach you how to identify the seasons:

" And of the children of Issachar, which were men that had understanding of the times, t know what Israel ought to do...."(1 Chronicles 12: 32)

Welcome to the *school of the Issachars*. The Principal will tell you something like the following:

"Welcome aboard. We belong to a group of people who know no defeat. The reason is that that we look up to the one who is in control of the weather. Because we look up to Him, He grants us understanding into the times, we know when to sow and when to expect a harvest. We are never disappointed because we do not look for harvest in the sowing season and never do, we lack a yield during harvest because the sowing season cannot pass by us unawares. We refuse to be bothered by what goes on around us. We do not follow the crowd; we follow the divine wind; even the spirit of God. Therefore, there are no idle seasons; they are just different. The difficulty with handling them is knowing what to do and when. Many have given up at the sowing season because it is a very difficult season. Why? It is a lean season that calls for sowing what you could have eaten. Eating your seed brings a temporary satisfaction but sowing, whether physical sowing or any form of investment can overcome poverty, not only in your lifetime but also generations after. It is okay when you go through difficult times in this lean season. Your tears will fertilize your toil. As you bow down to sow do not forget this, it is like pouring out your tears. By harvest, you will have joy. Your body will be calling for ease and pleasure but wake up before the morning dew evaporates. The weather may feel chilly but do not forget that we do not overcome cold by changing the weather, which is not under our control anyway, but by planting the cotton that keeps us warm. We the children of Issachar have never thought of changing the weather but rather changing our attitudes. Pleasure, apathy procrastination is among the enemies of our school. Watch against these attitudes.

Many great men are products of our school. We do not make great men; we only nurture them. For its only God that makes people great. Strength comes from within; not external circumstances — BE STRONG."

What an orientation from the principal of the "School of The Issachars". Maybe your question is, "How can we realize the best time or abundant season and ensure that it remains the best? The following guidelines will help you:

CONSIDER THE STAGES OF LIFE

Life is considered to be made up of three active parts:

1. **LEARNING YEARS —** This stage belongs to the first 30 years. This means that latest by thirty there should be the winding-up of traditional education. Also, parental influence must give way to very personal decisions like marriage and other issues. These are years of dependence. They are years that prepare us for a fruitful future. It is the foundation of the rest of our lives. It is here that many successes and failures are hidden. It can be compared to the foundation of a building. Its wrong construction could be the reason for the crack at the top. It is both hidden and concrete in nature. Difficult to identify and too hardened to rectify if even the fault is identified. When this stage is also well constructed you are sure the good construction is also hardened. Train up a child the way he should go. And when he is old, he will not depart from it.(Proverbs 22:6)

    Now I say that the heir, as long as he is a child, does not differ at all from a slave, though he is a master of all, but is under guardians and stewards until the time appointed by the Father. (Galatians 4:1,2) These massages are in no doubt a perfect description of this stage of life. Parents who understand the implications of this stage of life are on their way to being good parents and children who also understand they need their parents and teachers most at this stage are bound to have a healthy future. So prominent is the need to train a child that the Bible seems not to leave it as the sole responsibility of the parents. Galatians 4:2 enjoins every responsible adult to be involved and that will make up for the guardians and stewards. This seems to emphasize the African proverb that states that the child belongs to the mother only when it is in the womb but when it is born it becomes a family affair. It is divinely ordained that every responsible adult must be conscious of appropriate child-raising.

2. **APLICATION YEARS —** These cover the next 30 years when people are now implementing, on the first-hand basis, what they have learnt over the previous 30 years. By now they may have become spouses or parents. They must take full responsibility of their own lives and also those of their dependents. One word that summarizes this stage is decision or priority. That brings us into the nitty gritty of time management. This stage is not so much a matter of hard work as it is prioritizing and making the right decisions and choices in life. This stage is the center of life. This is where real battles **of life** take place. This is where generational mistakes are made but more importantly this is where generational legacies are established. Here, when the enemy gets one person, he kills two birds with one stone. At this stage many men become heads of families, managers of departments and companies, bearers of new visions. If there be any cracks in foundational years, most often, this is where it shows. The tricky deal at this stage is that it is covered up by the pursuit of economic survival for the family. There is no other stage in life that time becomes as essential as this. Many at this stage calculate the time they left of life and what can be accomplished within the time available. If it is so concluded that one's life's dream cannot be achieved, then one has option of being realistic or becoming jittery in taking major life's decisions at this time. Many also struggle with the reality of aging. Could they have lived better than they have done? Some refuse to accept that their physical energy and their health have changed. This stage can either trigger a crisis or blessing depending on how it is handled.

3. **THE STAGE OF EXPERIENCE—** By this third stage which may not cover as many years as the first two in view of its relatively short life span. Applicable principles have become experience. Those at this stage of life, by both family and social status, have become grandparents or senior citizens, and therefore effective counselors. They, at this stage, have so much to offer because they have been with the chief examiner of life — **TIME.** Listen to David,

"I have been young, and now I am old; yet have I not seen the righteous forsaken, nor his seed begging for bread." (Psalm 37:25)

In other words, "Believe me; God's mercy towards the righteous has stood the test of time." It is, by all means, because of this Solomon admonishes the young to listen to their parents and generally the elderly. *(Proverbs 23:22).* God places more responsibilities on the aged and therefore expects excellence from them.

"Teach the order men to be temperate, worthy of respect, self-controlled, and sound in faith, in love and in endurance.

Likewise, teach the older women to be reverent in the way they live, not to be slanders or addicted to much wine, but teach what is good. Then they can train the younger women to love their husbands and children." (Titus 2: 2-4)

This is the giving stage. The third stage of life is a mine of wisdom. Those at this stage are said to have four eyes; two in front and two behind. They have a long past and they can predict the future with accurate understanding. They see in a day what a younger person will see in three months. Of courses we are talking about adults who have approached life with objectivity. Here, adults who have applied, to a certain appreciable level, ethical values and principles are those under discussion.

Unfortunately, many have played the role of adults at adolescence and therefore could not enjoy the monitoring that was to groom them for a fruitful old age and therefore has nothing special to offer at adulthood. Maturity is born out of nurturing, not notoriety.

One of the major reasons why many retards in maturity and progress is that they fail to make use of current nurturing facilities for a fruitful future. Many assume that things will automatically work tomorrow; forgetting that tomorrow is the continuation of today. Yesterday was the foundation of today, and today, the foundation of tomorrow. God has therefore placed structures on our way to help us develop for the subsequent stages of our lives. To miss the effective use of such structures is a disaster, especially during the childhood and youthful stages. We have already discussed that a child is to be trained. *(Proverbs 22:6)*

What kind of training are children to be offered? Is it sending our children to the best schools? In other words, are we only to offer them the best of secular education? Are we not also responsible to offer moral education of some sort? Yes, to all of the above. But more importantly the training that the Bible is referring to here, is the training in the fear of God:

"Remember now thy creator in the days of thy youth, while the evil days come not, nor the years draw nigh, when thou shall say, I have pleasure in them; while the sun, or the light, or the moon, or the stars be not darkened nor the clouds return after the

rain: in the day when the keepers of the house shall tremble, and the strong men shall bow themselves, and the grinders cease because they are few, and those that look out of the windows be darkened, and the doors shalt be shut in the streets, when the sound of the grinding is low, and he shall rise up at the voice of the bird, and all the daughters of music shall be brought low. (Ecclesiastes 12:3,4)

The above biblical passage tries to depict pictorially what happens when men are aging. The preacher here warns that because of what happens with age it is best for men to remember their creator when they are young. Why "remember"? Because that is the way they have been trained to go as children. They, at this stage, should "remember" or in other words, ***not depart from the fear of their creator***.

Childhood and youthfulness without God are therefore the greatest disaster the world has ever experienced. Because the other stages of life seriously depend on this experience. For the greatest element of human growth is godliness. That is the satisfaction of the human soul. For godliness with (which produces) contentment is great gain. *(1 Timothy 6:6)*

Lack of appropriate upbringings leads to slavery. No wonder most of the addiction problems can be traced to inappropriate nurturing at childhood:

"Now I say, that the heir, as long as he is a child, differeth nothing from a servant, though he be lord of all; but is under tutors and governors until the time..." (Gal 4:1,2)

Time produces the best, but only with the appropriate input. From the above passage, bondage can be explained as lack of growth. So many of the deliverance-related problems we go through can be taken care of in maturity. For maturity is the basis of fruitfulness. Bondage means inability, limitation, retardation. The reason why many cannot reach their full potentials is that there may have been, along the line, absence of the influence of 'tutors and governors' among whom are parents, teachers and pastors. This may be one of the reasons why the Bible recommends the honoring of our parents. *(Ephesian 6:1-3)* The blessing attached to the obedience of this command is the promise of long life. Long days here mean something more than ordinary long life; they also mean purposeful, fruitful living and achievement of life's full potential. Honor here does not only mean respect but also appreciating and making the best use of good parental influence. I do not need to emphasize the negative effects broken homes have on children. Those children, who enjoy good parental influence generally, turn out to be more confident than those who do not. Not only in the area of confidence but all other areas including the choice of friends, personal discipline, general perception of life and related spiritual issues. Nurturing at a young age is therefore a life booster.

The child or the youth is therefore to submit to parents not only as a duty but also as a way of life. Many times, submission sounds like parents are being done a service; no, it is one of God's major channels for stabilizing us in life. Parents are also to understand that parenthood is not lordship but a responsibility from God. Some parents, by their lifestyles, have given the youth a "justification" to disobey them.

Bad parenting is the beginning of a chain of many mishaps that affects the victim's ability to become a good parent him/herself. Many good parents are simply beneficiaries of exemplary parenting.

Good parenting, apart from been elements of personal growth, is also a legacy. The children who miss positive parental influence are in danger of becoming bad parents themselves. Godly parenting therefore is an inheritance for generations ahead. Similarly, bad parenting is the woes of future generations.

It is important however to state that there is no stage in life where growth ends. And therefore, even after a good childhood and youthful experience, we are to continue growing into full maturity and responsible adulthood. Whilst we may have graduated from total parental oversight we enter into parallel relationships like marriage and many others like being follow members of the body of Christ. We may not see all these as good time investments, but they are. Husbands and wives are to love and submit respectively to each other. We have been taught that men are to love, and women are to submit. In other words, our concept of submission in this context is something different from love.

The prefix "sub" means under or lower. Paul therefore uses the two words to emphasize the different positions of the husband and wife. Specifically, they are to love each other from different positions or angles. The man is to love the wife as a man should and the wife should love the husband as a woman should. Humanity's primary need is two-fold; to love and to be loved. Whosoever cannot love has such a tremendous need, for love is the measurement of maturity. By loving our spouses, we grow. This is so important that the Bible says if we do otherwise, our prayers will be hindered. God has indicated the superiority of love over prayer in his word.

Considering the important of prayer as outlined in biblical passages like *1 Thess. 5:17* and *Luke 18:1*, love must be of utmost importance. The wise therefore is the one who spends his time to love. For love will surely endure and outrun time:

"And now abideth, faith, hope, charity(love), these three: but the greatest is love. Charity (love) never faileth: but whether there be prophecies, they shall fail: but whether there be tongues, they shall cease; whether there be knowledge, it shall vanish"(1 Corinthians 13:8, 13)

We are, in no way, limiting the practice of love to only married couples. However here is an area that real love goes through an effective test. It is so easy to play "loving" in a church environment, but it is not as easy at home. That is why many church leaders seem to succeed at church but encounter difficulties at home... We nevertheless need church as s parallel influence not only as adults but also through our entire lives.

The aged are not left out in the need for a support system. Old age is the most responsible stage in life. Many, at old age look back to assess their lives. Life at this time may be quite boring. There is retirement, children may be gone, and ill health may take its toll. But as much as these have needs, the younger generations need them the more. Why? They have so much of life's experience to impart. Besides, they prepare us for old age in our own lives, in the future. They teach us to place premium on the essentials of life; and by so doing use the life and time God has given us effectively. At this stage many, both the aged and the young, appreciate the importance of family life. For happy children and loving grandchildren are a social facility at old age that, apart from all else, slows down weariness and other handicaps that accompany old age.

It is important for all to understand that no age is without responsibility and the earlier we played according to the rules of the game of properly timing our lives, the better.

Dr Leslie Weather head in his book 'Time for God' has mathematically calculated a schedule which compares a lifetime of 70 years with hours of a simple day from seven in the morning to eleven in the night.

If your age is

15, the time is 10:25am

20, the time is 11:34am

25, the time is 12:42am

30, the time is 1:51pm

35, the time is 3:00pm

40, the time is 4:08pm

45, the time is 5:16pm

50, the time is 6:25pm

55, the time is 7:34pm

60, the time is 8:42pm

65, the time is 9:51 pm

70, the time is 11:00pm

CHAPTER 4

REDEEMING THE TIME

You often hear many say, ***"I do not have time".*** As much as some of such statements may be a true reflection of their busy schedules, many are in such states simply because they are not using their times wisely. A key reason for waste is when we lack the ability to, in a way, measure or taking full control of our resources. We can effectively take control of our time by planning with a pen and a paper. There is an element of covenanting in writing. In other words, issues that appear on paper have more potential to bind than those we simply think of. Isn't it interesting, that God wrote the Ten Commandments? His general covenant with the Jewish nation is a written code. Concerning the New Covenant of grace, God promises to write it in the heart of the believer. *(Jeremiah 31:31-34)* If God, the Almighty recognizes the power of the pen, our lives will be very effective if we develop the practice of plotting our daily activities on paper. If we commit ourselves to the things we write, distractions will fail to blur our visions and focus. The following guidelines are therefore to help you manage your time wisely. However, they will not matter if the goals these guidelines produce are not written on paper:

- **PLANNING CREATIVELY**

To time one's life is to plan it. It is to arrange life's resources and activities in such a way that there will be a clear action plan. This plan must also contain clear direction. By direction we are talking about being able to identify the most effective way or process by which one can achieve his goals. Your question may be how do I identify an effective way to achieve my goals?

You must look at where there are fewer hindrances. In other words, which way provides more resources or is less demanding when it comes to cost. Planning is arranging one's resources in a way that one can achieve his goals. If we fail to plan, we fail to achieve even the obviously achievable. We most often fail in life not because we deserve to fail but because we failed to match up our resources with our need. We failed to explore the options. There are many ways to success; even from a poor start. We are often not creative in our planning and setting of goals.

Many times, people plan on the resources they do not have; We plan the other person's way. Kofi did it this way and it worked for him. If I want to achieve what Kofi achieved, I must do it exactly Kofi's way. Kofi may have resources you do not have so if you decide its Kofi's way, you are bound to fail. It is to unfortunate many want to do things the other person's way. The challenge is that many times, success sanctifies a process and we all adore a particular process with pride that we feel pressured to achieve our goals the same way. We often look at the end and justify the means. The fact that one succeeded through a means does not mean it is the best. Yours may be better.

People therefore feel bad and uneasy if they do not find themselves in line with the accepted process. Many fail themselves too early because they have come to accept the fact that there is only one acceptable way to success.

I remember when we were in secondary school; Our old Scripture Union brethren who have completed school will come and guide us as to the various educational means to acquire a profession. At a certain stage, all of us had thought that going straight to the University was the only ladder to future success. At the time we had only few Universities in the country and university education was quite restricted and very competitive. But these old brethren, we call them, will come and enlighten us about the Agriculture colleges, the Teacher Trainings, the Nursing Trainings and other tertiary programs. They helped us to find out that some of the alternative programs can still get one to the University later in an easier way and at a better financial condition.

One major problem is that many are raised to explain education as a certificate and further explained education as only the formal or traditional type. Until recently we did not have many distance programs. There were a few educational opportunities even for workers to upgrade themselves. Today, education has become available in many ways and yet people are not making use of the easier options. Because we have over highlighted only one form of education- the straight formal university program many would do everything to enter even though they cannot afford.

People do not think about acquiring a basic income generating skill, work to raise some money and then pursue higher education. "Because my friends will laugh at me if they hear I did not attend the university", they will say. Do you know you can acquire a skill that will help you generate income when you enter the university? Life must be planned for creatively, especially in these difficult days that we live. There are a number of factors involved in formulating an effective plan. **For you to easily**

remember, the following acronym making up the word REACH will help in developing five factors for effective planning.

- **RESOURCE**

One must carefully assess resources available for every goal to be met. Resourcefulness does not only involve money; it also involves skill or know-how. This is where training becomes necessary. Training helps one to accomplish his goals mentally. Training takes the mind to one's level of success. Training opens one's life to the domain of possibilities.

One must also be able to assess the financial requirements for a given goal. The Bible admonishes a builder to assess the cost before he begins a project (Luke 14:28). To complete a project successfully one must be able to attach financial value to a project. A budget is but a goal in financial terms. Finance is one of the key restraints to the successful completion of every project. To be able to assess the weight of a goal to be achieved, in financial terms, is halfway through overcoming a major constraint. A serious person is therefore the one who is able to effectively evaluate the resource requirements of a goal. A goal cannot be said to be realistic if one cannot identify resources available in accomplishing it.

- **ENTRUST**

People are another key factor in effective planning. One sure way of achieving one's goal is to be a major contributor to the goal. Over dependence on others can adversely affect the certainty of a goal being achieved. On the other hand, there are components of projects and goals that need to be delegated or entrusted into the hands of other persons. If that aspect is also not clearly identified, it can lead to failure. Failure to identify the roles others can play in our pursuit of life goals can be a disaster. We must depend on God for the ability to trust someone to be part of our life and goals. A key part of planning therefore is to be able to identify people who can be part of our life's goals in terms of helping us achieve.

- **ARRANGE**

Having identified resources to REACH your goal and having identified people you can entrust with some aspects and also look up to, to have those aspects of your goal achieved, the next is to arrange them in order of priority. Doing so identifies goals that are urgent and those that can wait. There are goals that when achieved, make the achievement of subsequent others easier.

It does not mean that other goals down the ladder are not important; what it means is that you, as an individual, cannot achieve all your goals at once. Your limitations must teach you that you do not have all the resources to achieve all your goals. By arranging your goals in the order of priorities what you are actually doing is transforming some of your goals into resources so that they will in turn help you achieve others. A goal is never achieved until it becomes a resource for achieving other goals.

There is therefore the need to skillfully arrange one's goals functionally so that the achievement of one lead to the achievement of the other. Another way of arranging one's goal in order of priority is to identify the urgent ones. Urgent are the things one cannot afford to leave undone. The reason many procrastinate is that the activity lying at the top of the ladder can be done at any time. When it so happens, people are not motivated into action. To overcome procrastination, one must be able to carefully assess what vacuum or deficit will be created in his life, or others, if he or she does not perform the task today. There are needs that people endure at the peril of their lives. God Himself had said in His word that because a certain time will be very difficult, He will shorten it so that His own people will not lose their faith (Matthew 24: 22)

In Ghana, one of the few times we perform tasks promptly is when there are a major accident and people have died as a result. Many years ago, there was a tunnel filled with water but uncovered in between the dual carriage at the community one side of Tema Senior High School where I was a student. This underground cable tunnel was left uncovered till someone drove his new Peugeot 504 into it. The car sat in the pool with the driver inside the car. It took some time to get Harbor Fire Service to get to the scene and it took another amount of time to drain the water before the man was pulled out by a rope. I personally believe that under this condition, even if one had three chances to live, he or she would have still exhausted it all. The man died and by the following day, the tunnel had been covered. That is Ghana. We many times rise up only when life is lost. To us, it is easier to pay mortuary fees than to buy medicine, easier to buy a coffin than to give shelter. Your goal is the hope for another. Rise up to achieve.

Another way to arrange your goals is to look at the realistic as against the unrealistic.

One reason why a goal may be unrealistic today is that it can be classified as a long-term goal. Achieving them may not be possible today but may be tomorrow. Early on, we had stated that one achieved goal can become a resource for the achievement of another goal. Why should one exhaust his energy on a goal that is not achievable? Hardly achievable goals serve as obstacles to achieving other goals. It is better to aim at a small goal and to achieve it than to concentrate on unrealistic goals. The small goal you can achieve is better than the big one that cannot be achieved. Faith must be livable. The just shall live by faith (Hebrews 10:38).

It is therefore wise to break down bigger goals into smaller units so they can have achievable components. Imagine what will happen if school from pre-school to university is chained up in a long line of let's say classes 1-16. Breakdown your goals into smaller units and make them achievable.

- **CONDITION**

Encarta Dictionary explains condition as to make strong, healthy, and ready; to give somebody or something a treatment to improve general health, soundness, readiness for life, appearance or performance. Here we are looking at apportioning time effectively. Do important things at the prime time. Do most difficult or important tasks at such a time that its demands can be met. Life can be very cumbersome when it is not well arranged. Many times, we do not carefully assess how our personal programs work but rather follow what others are doing.

There is however the best time of the day, the best day of the week or the stage in life that a task can be effectively accomplished. One must be cautioned that such time demarcations cannot be made without creating the perimeter for commencements and deadlines. Setting deadlines create urgency and also eradicate procrastination. It has been stated quite a number of times through this book that all things will not effectively prosper at all times. There is the best time for everything, and the best time is the time with the most appropriate conditions.

Many times, our best time assigned for a particular task is intruded into by less important and the unexpected; they still demand their share of time. They come up with demands you cannot put on the shelf. One main solution to this is to identify unexplored times into which such demands can be placed. The following are time fragments that are mostly unexplored;

1. **Leisure Hour**
Such times can be identified as times one is in a queue be it for transport and for an enquiry. Such times can be used for reading assignments or used for important phone calls to be made.

2. **TV Time**
Many times, we sit in front of the TV not knowing what to expect but keep watching to see if an interesting program will appear. To water down the importance of television in our personal lives is a fallacy. Only few can do without it. At least one would want to listen to news, to watch an interesting film or episode, to listen to music or watch a documentary However, one must commit himself TV by plan. Put it on by program and when done put off. In between TV programs are many adverts. Most often the same adverts or jingles are played over and over. By the second or third time you must determine whether the details of these adverts matter to you or not. Even if they matter, the next is to look at one's plan of action and then stop watching it. Go ahead and watch your film or soap opera but when the adverts begin to use the time for something important. You can have a book by your side and read any time the advert starts.

3. **Delays**
Most of us who live in our Africa accept delays graciously. Unfortunately, most programs or ceremonies can start any time within the next one hour or more of a scheduled time. I had to attend a wedding that was to start at 12:00 noon. In fact, I left the house a few minutes to the time though the venue was about one and a quarter hour drive. I had become nervous because I had a role on the program. If I had the money, I would have paid any amount to get a taxi to take me to the venue without delay. Because I did not have enough money, I decided to go by regular transport. I got there at 2:00pm and the place was empty. I got so embarrassed thinking. I had disappointed the couple because the program was over. Believe you me it had not started. We had to wait one more hour before the wedding started at 3:00pm. Some program organizers will time the program one hour earlier to forestall such unacceptable behavior. A small book on you or those who carry their laptops can always work when delays arise. Delays can be very frustrating to a busy person. Carry assignments in your bag because 'delay' is a CHERISHED citizen of Africa.

4. **Bathroom & Toilet**

   Can you fix a radio somewhere in your bathroom so you can listen to news? Is there anywhere in your toilet you can paste reminders? Can you create any box in the toilet where you can place your devotionals and read them every morning you visit the toilet?

5. **Cooking Time & Mealtime**

   These days most of our Church sermons are taped and many books are beginning to be put on audios. Or one can record lectures in class and play when cooking. Sermons could be listened to or even family devotions done at mealtime. There are many other explored times based on one's personal activities - traffics and even hospital admissions can be blessings in disguise if the time is well explored.

6. **HAMMER**

   Hit hard at your goals. Aims do not descend, they are attained. Aims must be pursued decisively. We must be committed to our aspirations. Commitment pays off. The reason why many hardly achieve anything is that they give up too early. Life calls for persistence. Many want easy means to achieve goals. There are only a few easy paths to success and those ones are already occupied by many. To use this crowded road, one may have to stay in a queue forever.

Sent by the Church of Scotland to Africa as a missionary - physician, Dr. David Livingstone served for more than three decades. A South Africa mission society wrote to Livingstone that they had some good men they would like to send over to assist him …. They asked if there was a good road to where Livingstone was currently serving.

Livingstone wrote back to the society: "If you have men who will come only if they knew the good road, I don't need them. I need men who will come even if there is no road." To many successes, there is no easy road. Persistence in the face of challenges and difficulties is the word.

There aren't any hard-and-fast rules for getting ahead in the; just hard ones. "When I was a young man", says George Bernard Shaw, "I realized that nine of the ten things I did were failures. I didn't want to be a failure, so I did ten more work.

"One day, while idly viewing a display of life preservers in a faction window, he became obsessed with an idea which was to change his life. The material employed in making those life preservers was very limited, because it was considerably unstable. The young man, however, was fascinated. Surely there was a great future in that product; all it needed was the right man to perfect.

With characteristic optimism and no knowledge of chemistry, he began a series of experiments. He melted the gummy substance on the kitchen stove and fascinated hundreds of shoes which he stored away in a shed. When the weather turned hot his nose quickly told him that he had failed as the odor of the melting shoes carried for miles? Undaunted he continued his experiment, combining every ingredient he could use to make the gum stabilize. But each time he thought he had found an answer, it turned into disappointment. Then one day, as it happened with so many discoveries throughout history, a lucky accident occurred. While working with still another formula, some of the substance spilled on the hot stove. Instead of melting, it charred and hardened. Success was at last within his grasps. After a lifetime devoted to an idea which had indeed become a mania, he had accidentally developed the process which will later be called vulcanization. This single development led directly to the establishment of one of the world's great industrial giants …. He helped to establish the rubber industry in America. Charles Goodyear... Moses, Gene, America's Great, Alpha venture New York. 1975

WATCH TIME WASTERS

❖ **Worry**
Worry displaces effectiveness. Purposefulness, on the other hand, displaces worry. The way to worry is to worry. In Joshua chapter One, God said the following to Joshua:

"Moses my servant is dead; now therefore arise, go over this Jordan, thou(you), and all this people, unto the land which I do give to them,"(Joshua 1:2)

God, in this passage was telling Joshua that Moses was my servant first before he became your master and therefore, I also have a funeral. But we have a goal to achieve; life must go on. Therefore, be up and doing. Worry hardly goes by itself; it must be displaced with positive activity. Get up and do something positive.

❖ Laziness

There is no situation in this life as tiring as laziness. There lazy person is always tired. Laziness wears one out. Activity prepares the body for more activity. Poverty is not necessarily lack of money but the inability to meet reoccurring needs. The first step towards meeting our needs is rising up with the intention to do so. The closest link to the feet are the eyes though the two are far apart; we see well with "standing feet". Many want to see before they get up; that is why many remain seated. God does not fix his lamp by our eyes; He fixes them by our feet; Until we get up to 'walk', we will not see light. His light is available for the 'feet' that creates a path. Of course, we are not just talking about physical feet but rather the mind that makes a move.*(Psalm 119:105)*

❖ Absent Mindedness

This can be described as double mindedness. This is a situation where one's mind and the "hands" do not belong to the same place. Hands here stand for work or a particular activity. Absent mindedness can also be described as lack of concentration. This happens many times when we are not interested in what we are doing or when excellence is not our set goal for doing what we do. That is why we should engage the mind before we start working.

❖ Lack of Planning

Planning is doing the job on paper. By planning obstructions can be removed before the real job is started. Efficiency does not only mean producing the best results, it also means the results coming in a stipulated time. Planning makes you your own supervisor; the most efficient way to success.

❖ Suppositions and Chances

Doing things without any expectation and not being certain of what to expect can be very disastrous. One cannot put in his maximum because of fear of no returns. This is the   danger of the lottery. The want for the quick success is the reason for the pursuit of chances. But the only way to true success is hard work. 'Short cuts' are dangerous.

❖ Delays

A delay in one area affects many other areas. Many of the delays come as a result of circumstances beyond our control. However, many delays can be predicted and therefore dealt with ahead of time. The possibility of power failures calls for ironing one's clothing ahead of time. The possibility of car breakdowns calls for setting out early enough to make up for any of such eventualities.

Many times, you hear passengers scream when the bus runs out of fuel. It makes sense to go with an earlier bus knowing the kind of buses in which we ride in Africa. Plan to be at meeting, at work, or at school at least 15 minutes before time. It will help you get ready and concentrated.

❖ Envy

Envy directs all our attention on what the other person is doing. Not because one wants to learn something from the other but because one is obsessed with the success of another that he cannot concentrate on his personal goals. Envy causes people to try to do what others can do better and not what they themselves can do more excellently. Many can be overwhelmed by others' achievements that they can hardly have any "space" in their minds about their own achievements. When such a thing happens to people, they begin to see themselves as failures though in one way or the other they could attain success. All their concentration is on the other person. In this way they will lack motivation to pursue their own life's goals. There is this interesting video that was shared on the Facebook title *"My Shoes"* A boy with tattered shoes and often laughed at passionately wanted to be like another sitting nearby with a beautiful pair of shoes. His wishes were granted, and he immediately became the other boy with those pair of beautiful shoes and smart clothing only to be trapped in a disabled pair of legs whilst the other jumps around happily in those tattered shoes but newly empowered legs. We are all abled in one way and disabled in another. Others' disabilities are not as obvious as yours. That does not mean those do not exist. Neither does it mean they are not as bordering as yours. Envy and discontentment can deny us fruitful and creative moments that God has endowed us with. There is a vast domain of opportunities.

❖ Unidentified procedures

When appropriate procedures are not outlined, haphazard results are produced and when that happens there can never be an effective means of trouble shooting when a problem arises. One of the greatest threats in life is when one cannot identify the source of his problems; it is tantamount to beating the air in an attempt to solve our problems.

Complex projects or goals must be broken down into simpler and easily identifiable units. It is said that profundity is not born out of complexity but rather, simplicity. This raises the need for training and education. Yes, education and training can be time consuming but, in the end, it is time and resources saving. This also robes in leadership, mentoring and effective orientation to produce a once and for all excellence. There is so much hardship in many parts of the world, so time is not taken to learn and do things the right way and many have not exercised their creative instincts enough to arrange systems and procedures effectively. Starting well can be less stressful that rectifying a hazard or an accident. Resources are costly, they should not be wasted through ignorance.

WORK DISTRACTORS TO BE CHECKED.

Work is one of the gifts God has given us to help us improve upon life. Work improves the quality of the life God has given unto us. In other words, work is the continuation of God's creative purposes and processes. God gives us life in a seed form, and we are to nurture it into growth and fruitfulness. To explain further, life is like a raw material, we have been given the responsibility to finish up the process. One area that calls for time investment is work.

Many work so hard but their efforts lack projections. They cannot define the exact thing they want at the end of the work; neither can they define when they want that done. Many are 'workers' without performing any targeted task. All they are doing is working somehow. Only few in this life perspire towards perfection. Many work in exchange for more energy to work again. To be blunt, they work for food. But life is more than food. Many people do not care about what they do as long as they are paid. We do not work to get paid; we work to complete God's process of creation. Work therefore does not center only around energy but also on creativity. We therefore need to fine-tune our attitude towards work. In our part of the world, work has been choked by so many unfavorable factors. Management 'gurus' can outline a host of such obstacles to efficient work. I am outlining the following purely from experience and a layman's view.

☐ **Cumbersome arrangement of tools and Equipment**

A situation like this inhibits a lot of progress. A well-arranged office and a good secretary or storekeeper will be of much help. Many churches and Christian organizations have overlooked this area for their own peril. Many man-hours can be spent searching for files and tools. A professional approach, as already stated, is a key solution.

☐ **Undivided Labor**

This is a situation where everybody will attempt to do the same thing that can be done by one person, for the apparent reward for a particular assignment or because a particular task may be less risky. There is therefore the need for conscious delegation of assignments and putting in place, supervisory structures...

Another good reason for the need of assigned labor is that constant attachment to one task by the same person may create a certain form of specialization and therefore the possibility of efficiency in terms of time and quality. This may have some disadvantages of course but that cannot be compared to a situation where everybody is waiting for a prompt before an action is taken.

☐ **Lack of Safety Measures**

Accidents are strong impediments to effectiveness. Time will not wait for the accident victim because he is injured; time waits for no man. Maximum safety must be ensured to keep progress steady. People should not expose themselves to hazardous situations. It is said that accidents do not happen, they are caused. We always pass by hazards unconcerned until there is a disaster. We only sit up after precious lives and properties are lost. Accidents are to be prevented, not to be witnessed. The Ghanaian prides himself in saying that when the accident happened, he was a witness. Even the Christian does not see God keeping us from trouble as a miracle; it is only a miracle when He saves us from trouble. God is happy to see us do well and be in good health. (3John:2) We keep His will by keeping ourselves from unnecessary dangers. I am not saying there will not be troubles, what I am saying is that we should not create our own problems.

☐ Lack of Social Amenities

When workers have to travel long distances for food during break, then the purpose of the break loses its value because there is no rest: workers resume already tired. Other workers will have to wake up too early so as to get to work on time. When workers begin the day with many frustrations, they add to the problems of their organizations instead of being part of the solution. Those who nevertheless begin well may get tired too soon. Productivity should not be measured by how much human energy is spent but rather how much of it is saved. True work builds up, it does not waste away. Social amenities should be provided for workers to make office breaks purposeful.

☐ Lack of Appropriate Resources

Essential resources ought to be in stock. Prompt availability of resource is a plus to efficiency. This is what makes planning imperative. Resources should be gathered for impending projects.

This is an area that many overlooks. At times we think that projects must be started, and one will identify the needs with time. No, gathering resources is a strong indication that one definitely identifies the dimensions of an assignment or a project. Waiting to identify resources needed is a strong indication that the supervisor of the project is the project itself and not the human supervisor. When such a situation happens operators cannot be in control of projections because an arising need for resources will be the final determiner. David, one of the greatest leaders Israel ever had, keenly understood the essentiality of gathering resources for a task before it really begins:

"Furthermore, David the King said unto all the congregation, Solomon my son, whom alone God hath chosen, is yet young and tender, and work is great: for the palace is not for man, but for God. Now I have prepared with all my might for the House of my God the gold for things to be made gold, and the silver for things of silver, and the brass for the things of brass, the iron for the things of iron, and wood for the things of wood; onyx stones, and stones to be set, glistering stones, and of divers colors, and all manner of precious stones, and marble stones in abundance".(I Chronicles 29:1, 2).

How could David understand that his son Solomon was too young for the task? By the magnitude of logistics gathered for temple. At times necessity can make us start many projects without gathering or making room for all the resources. However, they should be planned for.

☐ Sickness

Whosoever holds a task dearer than his health may not live to see it completed. The work that such individuals think cannot be suspended, stops because they soon breakdown. Some possible ways to prevent being sick are cleanliness, good dieting and rest. Satan operates best where there is filth. Look at those possessed by Satan; they are either physically or morally filthy. To live physically healthy, people should be both physically and morally clean.

The need for good dieting is supported by the fact that the first medication God prescribed for man was food. *(Genesis 1::29)* After God had defined the workload of man in *Genesis 1:28,* the next thing God mentioned was the available sources of food. *(Genesis 1::29)* whoever fails in following this prescription obeys the medical doctor's prescription in vain. God's direction for the consumption of any nutrient is found in

Ecclesiastes 10:17: "Blessed are you, o land whose king is of noble birth and whose princes eat at a proper time for strength and not for drunkenness."(NIV)

The two very important principles guiding every consumption of food substance are that, consumption must be for strength and also must be done at the proper time. This confirms the fact that one must eat to live and not live to eat. Whoever does not have appropriate times for eating is in trouble. We must not wait to be very hungry to eat. We should, when it is time to do so.

☐ Burn Out

God Himself believes in rest. He rested from all His work on the seventh day. He also commanded the Israelites to rest on the seventh day. The importance of rest can be derived from the fact that our eternal salvation is compared to rest. *(Mathew 11:28; Hebrews 4:9-11)* How valuable is rest to God? God gave us the responsibility of work not because His power is limited, but because he wants us to be part of His creational process. As much as god abhors laziness, He does not want us to take the world upon ourselves as if without us the world will fall and crack. Rest is an indication that we are limited as humans and there is the need for us, by resting, to practice depending on God in faith. Resting or standing still creates room for the miraculous. *(Exodus 14:14)*

Rest also heals our mental faculties to freshen up for deeper thinking. A certain level of tiredness does not allow intellectual efficiency. God's recommended pattern of rest was based on time and not according to how tired one is. If it gets to the seventh day, rest

(Exodus 20:8-11). People are not to rest only because they are tired but also because it is the scheduled time to rest. That is why God created day and night; day for work, night for rest. Modern economics is nullifying the day / work and night / rest system but that never takes away the need for bodily rest. The problem with many is that they want to feel tired before they rest. But as much as some work may have gone on, an amount of energy is exerted even if one does not feel it. On many occasions, the day an individual will really feel tired, the situation has already gotten out of hand. The same principle applies to eating; one does not eat only because he is hungry but because it is time to eat. Whether one feels hungry or not, the food he ate eight hours ago must have been digested, all things being equal. We need to constantly revitalize our energy base for efficiency by taking our eating habits and resting patterns very seriously.

Work must be seen as a natural part of life, not because nothing will be done without our active involvement. God, and therefore the world, has many like us who can do the work better than we do. Many hard-working people have died, and others have continued from where they abruptly left off. You and your dependents are the only persons who lose when you die before your time; Work does not.

Progress is made up of movements and stops. The fact that one is not stopping does not necessarily mean that he is being progressive. Stops are good for rest, refreshments, assessments, projections, transitions etc. Workaholism

CONCLUSION

TRUE WISDOM

Wisdom is a very vast concept. There are a lot of indicators of wisdom in this life. In other words, one can identify the wise by how they respond to various situations. However, there are key indicators that cut across. Such indicators reflect in the life of almost every wise person. One of such is the effective handling of time. The Bible has, on a number of occasions, associated foolishness with inappropriate use of time:

"See then that ye walk circumspectly, not as fools, but as wise redeeming the time because the days are evil. Where, be ye not unwise, but understanding what the will of the Lord is." (Ephesians 5:15-17).

"So, teach us to number our days, that we may apply our hearts unto wisdom." (Psalm 90:12).

"The Kingdom of heaven be likened unto ten virgins, which took their lamps, and went forth to meet the bridegroom. And five of them were wise, and five were foolish. They that were foolish took their lamps and took oil with them. But the wise took oil in their vessels with their lamps. While the bridegroom tarried, they all slumbered and slept. And at midnight there was a cry, 'Behold, the bridegroom cometh; go ye out meet Him.' Then all those virgins arose and trimmed their lamps. And the foolish said unto the wise, 'Give us of your oil; for our lamps are gone out.' But the wise answerer saying 'not so; Lest there be not enough for us and you; but go ye rather to them that sell and buy for yourselves.'
And while they went to buy, the bridegroom came; and they that were ready went in with him to the marriage; and the door was shut.
After, came also the other virgins, 'Lord, Lord open to us.' But He answered and said, 'verily, I say unto you, I know you not.' Watch therefore, for ye know neither the day nor the hour wherein the son of man cometh." (Mathew 25;1-13).

All of the passages above link time with wisdom. The first passage from Ephesians contains the following words: fools, wise, unwise, time. The second from psalm also contain, days, wisdom. The third and the longest contain words like; wise, foolish, tarried (delayed), midnight, ready, watch, day, and hour.

Many have read a lot of meaning into the third passage. The meaning normally centers on what extra oil in the passage mean. To some it is prayerlessness; to others it is the absence of the holy Spirit in one's life; to others still, it is lack of anointing since oil is a symbol of the Holy Spirit. It is true, we as Christians, are lamps and in burning, we need constant refilling to keep shining. In this passage the lack of extra oil is not as unfortunate situation as the fact that they did not have the oil at the time they needed it. For the lamp-oil phenomenon indicates that with constant burning the oil will run out and therefore the need to refill.

The bridegroom delayed. The delay, I believe was to give these virgins adequate time to prepare. It was time to check their lamps and to round up preparations. However, they chose to sleep instead. This happens to all of us; instead of making good use of delays, we complain and curse and at other time, do nothing. Of course, the wise ones slept appropriately because, after all, they had finished their task. But the foolish ones slept when it was not time to.

The bridegroom, though delayed, still came to meet the five virgins not ready. What an unfortunate situation! They, there and then, realized that they had not made adequate preparation. The otherwise ones only had enough for themselves. In response to the encouragement by the others, they went back into the city to get oil. They actually succeeded in getting some, but they got it at the time the door to the marriage feast was closed. They knocked and called but the door had been closed. Unfortunate!

Jesus' own interpretation of this parable clearly states that he was talking about time. *"Watch ye therefore, for ye know neither the day nor the hour wherein the son of man cometh."*

One of the most painful situations in life comes when one realizes that he had every opportunity to have accomplished a task and still failed to accomplish it. It is not as bad as when one recognizes that he tried his best with the available resources and yet failed to achieve an aim. Such, though sad, can console themselves with the fact that their best was not good enough.

The foolish virgins, by missing out on effective use of time, missed what they may have spent a considerable amount of time to prepare for. You may call it an important life goal. Because of their inability to make use of a delay that may have spanned just a moment of time, they missed what they may been preparing for over a long period of time. If our goals are not linked to appropriate timing, they may lose their values. Yes, God is a God of the second chance but by that, God does not mean we should blow up the opportunities that come our way at their most appropriate times. By giving us a second opportunity, he is not downplaying the importance of timing.

There are so many things you can do best do now: if you are a student, it is time to study; not 'practice' marriage. If your children are in school, it is now time to invest in their lives and stop 'chasing' others' daughters. Many wished they had taken care of their children whilst they had the opportunity to do so; but this realization comes so strong on their deathbed; too late. If you have a friend, a spouse or a relation to forgive, it is now. You can't wait. Urgency is the biblical approach to reconciliation:

"Therefore, if you bring your gift to the altar, and there remember that your brother has something against you, leave your gift there before the altar and go your way. First be reconciled to your brother and come and offer your gift."(Mathew 5:23)

Offering can be postponed but forgiveness should not. Forgive now. Today is the day of salvation. Do not wait till tomorrow to give over your life to Jesus. Forsake your sinful way now before it is too late. You have today to do that. Tomorrow does not belong to you. You do not control your life.

The following article appeared in Gospel Herald:

"An earnest Christian doctor one day called to see an old man whom he frequently visited before. The old fellow was suffering from bronchitis. The doctor made necessary inquiries, and after promising to get some medicine ready when called for, he was about to say 'good-bye' when the patient's wife asked, 'When must John take the medicine, Sir? 'Let me see; you are not very ill; suppose you begin to take it month from today.' 'A month from today, sir?' they cried in astonishment. 'Yes, why not? Is that too soon? Too soon! Why sir? I may be dead then! Said the patient.

'This is true; but you must remember you really are not very bad yet. Still you had better begin to take it in a week.' 'But sir,' cried John in great perplexity, 'begging your pardon, but I might not live a week.' 'Of course, you may not John but very likely you will. And the medicine will be in the house; it will keep and if you find yourself getting worse you could take some. I shan't charge anything for it. If you should feel worse tomorrow than you could begin.' 'Sir I thought you would tell me to begin today.' 'Begin today by all means,' said the doctor, kindly. 'I only wanted to show you how false your reasoning is, when your put-off taking the medicine which the Great physician has provided for your sin-soul. Just think how long you have neglected the remedy he has provided. For years you have turned away from the Lord Jesus. You have said to yourself next week or next year,' or when I am on my deathbed, I will seek the Lord'; anytime rather the present.

And yet the present is the only time that you are sure of. God's offer is only for today. Remember, 'Now is the day of salvation. 'You may be dead tomorrow!'

"Behold now is the acceptable time; behold now is the day of salvation"(II Cor 6:2). The emphasis is on the "now". Too many people are place in the future their idea and hope of being right with God." But how close is anyone to "the end"? Who knows when the moment of accounting will be? Will we wait for a year, a month, a week, or even a day? Better to take the healing medicine now.

"Behold, now is the acceptable time, behold now is the day of salvation."
(II Corinthians 6:2). If you are ready now to accept the Lord Jesus Christ as your personal Savior

Makes the following your personal prayer:

Dear Father in Heaven, thank you for loving and caring for me. Thank you for doing something about my life through your son Jesus Christ. I am sorry for running my life. Forgive me for my hardheartedness. I now accept and receive Your gifts of Christ Jesus into my life. I declare Him as my Lord and savior. Grant me the joy and assurance of your salvation. Thank you, Father, for hearing my prayer and saving my life. Thank You for making me Your child. Amen...

Now that you have become a believer in Christ, find a good church to attend. A good church:

1. Preaches Christ and emphasizes salvation in Him alone.

2. Emphasizes holy Christian living.

3. Minister to the total man-is interested in people's spiritual, social and physical needs.

Also learn to pray always and study your Bible so that you can grow in the Lord. For further help write to:

Pastor William Okyere

Tel: +233 (0) 557 581 505

pneumeduf@gmail.com.

TIME SPAN AGES

TIME SPAN AGES 1-100
YOU HAVE LIVED ABOUT THIS MANY

AGE	MONTHS	DAYS	HOURS	MINIUTES	SECONDS
1	12	365	8,760	525,600	31,536,000
2	24	730	17,520	1,051,200	63,072,000
3	36	1,095	26,280	1,576,800	94,608,000
4	48	1,460	35,040	2,102,400	126,144,000
5	60	1,826	43,824	2,629,440	157,766,400
6	72	2,191	52,584	3,155,040	189,302,400
7	84	2,556	61,344	3,680,640	220,838,400
8	96	2,921	70,104	4,206,240	252,374,400
9	108	3,287	78,888	4,733,280	283,996,800
10	120	3,652	87,648	5,258,880	315,532,800
11	132	4,017	96,408	5,784,480	347,068,800
12	144	4,382	105,168	6,310,080	378,604,800
13	156	4,748	113,952	6,837,120	410,227,200
14	168	5,113	122,712	7,362,720	441,763,200
15	180	5,478	131,472	7,888,320	473,299,200
16	192	5,843	140,232	8,413,920	504,835,200
17	204	6,209	149,016	8,940,960	536,457,600
18	216	6,574	157,776	9,466,560	567,993,600
19	228	6,939	166,536	9,992,160	599,529,600
20	240	7,304	175,296	10,517,760	631,065,600
21	252	7,670	184,080	11,044,800	662,688,000
22	264	8,035	192,840	11,570,400	694,224,000
23	276	8,400	201,600	12,096,00	725,760,000
24	288	8,765	210,360	12,621,600	757,296,000
25	300	9,131	219,144	13,148,640	788,918,000
26	312	9,496	227,904	13,674,240	820,454,400
27	324	9,861	236,664	14,199,840	851,990,400
28	336	10,226	245,424	14,725,440	883,526,400

29	348	10,592	254,208	15,252,480	915,148,800
30	360	10,957	262,968	15,778,080	946,684,800
31	372	11,322	271,728	16,303,680	978,220,800
32	384	11,687	280,488	16,829,280	1,009,756,800
33	396	12,053	289,272	17,356,320	1,041,379,200
34	408	12,418	298,032	17,881,920	1,072,915,200
35	420	12,783	306,792	18,407,520	1,104,451,200
36	432	13,148	315,552	18,933,120	1,135,987,200
37	444	13,514	324,336	19,460,160	1,167,609,600
38	456	13,879	333,096	19,985,760	1,199,145,600
39	468	14,244	341,856	20,511,360	1,230,681,600
40	480	14,609	350,616	21,036,960	1,262,217,600
41	492	14,975	359,400	21,564,000	1,293,840,000
42	504	15,340	368,160	22,089,600	1,325,376,000
43	516	15,705	376,920	22,615,200	1,356,912,000
44	528	16,070	385,680	23,140,800	1,388,448,000
45	540	16,436	394,464	23,667,840	1,420,070,400
46	552	16,801	403,224	24,193,440	1,451,606,400
47	564	17,166	411,984	24,719,040	1,483,142,400
48	576	17,531	420,744	25,244,640	1,514,678,400
49	588	17,897	429,528	25,771,680	1,546,300,800
50	600	18,262	438,288	26,297,280	1,577,836,800
51	612	18,627	447,048	26,822,880	1,609,372,800
52	624	18,992	455,808	27,348,480	1,640,908,800
53	636	19,358	465,592	27,875,520	1,672,531,200
54	648	19,723	473,352	28,401,120	1,704,067,200
55	660	20,088	482,112	28,926,720	1,735,603,200
56	672	20,453	490,872	29,452,320	1,767,139,200
57	684	20,819	499,656	29,979,360	1,798,761,600
58	696	21,184	508,416	30,504,960	1,830,297,600
59	708	21,549	517,176	31,030,560	1,861,833,600
60	720	21,914	525,936	31,556,160	1,893,369,600
61	732	22,280	534,720	32,083,200	1,924,992,000
62	744	22,645	543,480	32,608,800	1,956,528,000

33	756	23,010	552,240	33,134,400	1,988,064,000
64	768	23,375	561,000	33,660,000	2,019,600,000
65	780	23,741	569,784	34,187,040	2,051,222,400
66	792	24,106	578,544	34,712,640	2,082,758,400
67	804	24,471	587,304	35,238,240	2,114,294,400
68	816	24,836	596,064	35,763,840	2,145,830,400
69	828	25,202	604,848	36,290,880	2,177,452,800
70	840	25,567	613,608	36,816,480	2,208,988,800
71	852	25,932	622,368	37,342,080	2,204,524,800
72	864	26,297	631,128	37,867,680	2,272,060,800
73	876	26,663	639,912	38,394,720	2,303,683,200
74	888	27,028	648,672	38,920,320	2,335,219,200
75	900	27,393	657,432	39,445,920	2,366,755,200
76	912	27,758	666,192	39,971,520	2,398,291,200
77	924	28,124	674,976	40,498,560	2,492,913,600
78	936	28,489	683,736	41,024,160	2,461,449,600
79	948	28,854	692,496	41,549,760	2,492,985,600
80	960	29,219	701,256	42,075,360	2,524,521,600
81	972	29,585	710,040	42,602,400	2,556,144,000
82	984	29,950	718,800	43,128,000	2,587,680,000
83	996	30,315	727,560	43,653,600	2,619,216,000
84	1,008	30,680	736,320	44,179,200	2,650,752,000
85	1,020	31,046	745,104	44,706,240	2,682,374,400
86	1,032	31,411	753,864	45,231,840	2,713,910,400
87	1,044	31,776	762,624	45,757,440	2,745,446,400
88	1,054	32,141	771,384	46,283,040	2,776,982,400
89	1,068	32,507	780,168	46,810,080	2,808,604,800
90	1,080	32,872	788,928	47,335,680	2,840,140,800
91	1,092	33,237	797,688	47,861,280	2,871,676,800
92	1,104	33,602	806,448	48,386,880	2,903,212,800
93	1,116	33,968	815,232	48,913,920	2,934,835,200
94	1,128	34,333	823,992	49,439,520	2,966,371,200
95	1,140	34,698	832,752	49,956,120	2,997,907,200
96	1,152	35,063	841,512	50,490,720	3,029,443,200

97	1,164	35,429	850,296	51,017,760	3,061,065,600
98	1,176	35,794	859,056	51,543,360	3,092,602,600
99	1,188	36,159	867,816	52,068,960	3,124,137,600
100	1,200	36,524	876,576	52,594,560	3,155,673,600